caring for us

I am an
Optician

Deborah Chancellor

Photography by Chris Fairclough

W

This edition 2012

First published in 2010
by Franklin Watts
338 Euston Road
London NW1 3BH

Copyright © Franklin Watts 2010

Franklin Watts Australia
Level 17/207 Kent Street
Sydney, NSW 2000

Series editor: Jeremy Smith
Art director: Jonathan Hair
Design: Elaine Wilkinson
Photography: Chris Fairclough

Every attempt has been made to clear copyright. Should there be any
inadvertent omission please apply to the publisher for rectification.

With thanks to Mohammed, Julia, Karen, Eleanor, Peter
and all the staff at Walden Opticians.

Dewey number: 617.7'52

ISBN: 978 1 4451 0906 0

Printed in China

Franklin Watts is a division of Hachette Children's Books,
an Hachette UK company.
www.hachette.co.uk

Contents

Words in **bold** are in the glossary on page 24.

My job

I am an optician.
I test people's sight,
and check that their
eyes are healthy.

What do you think?

Why is
it important
to have
healthy eyes?

4

I work at an optician's in a town
called Saffron Walden.

Taking calls

What do you think?

Who should go to the optician's for an eye test?

If people want an **eye test**, they phone the optician's to make an appointment.

My **receptionist** arranges appointment
times, and enters them on the computer.

My equipment

I have lots of equipment in my surgery, which I use to check my patients' eyesight.

Do you know?

You should eat plenty of green vegetables to keep your eyes healthy.

If my patients need glasses, I find **lenses** that are the right strength for them.

The waiting room

When my patients arrive for an eye test, they check in at the reception desk.

They sit in a waiting room until I am ready to see them.

11

Having an eye test

I like talking to my patients. I always explain to them what I am going to do in their eye test.

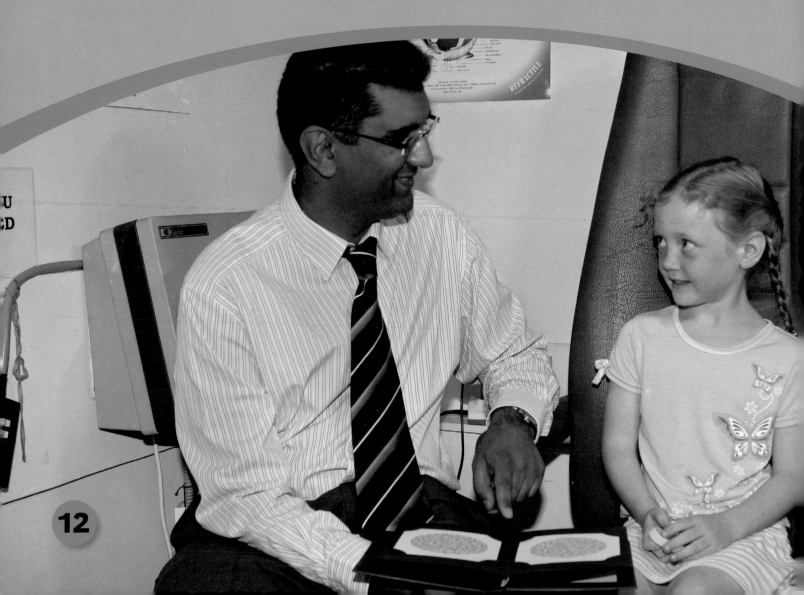

You should have your first eye test before you are one year old.

I ask my patients to look at different tests, and tell me what they can see clearly. I give children a sticker if they have been good!

13

Healthy eyes

I check that my patients' eyes are healthy. I test how well they can see with an instrument called an **ophthalmoscope**.

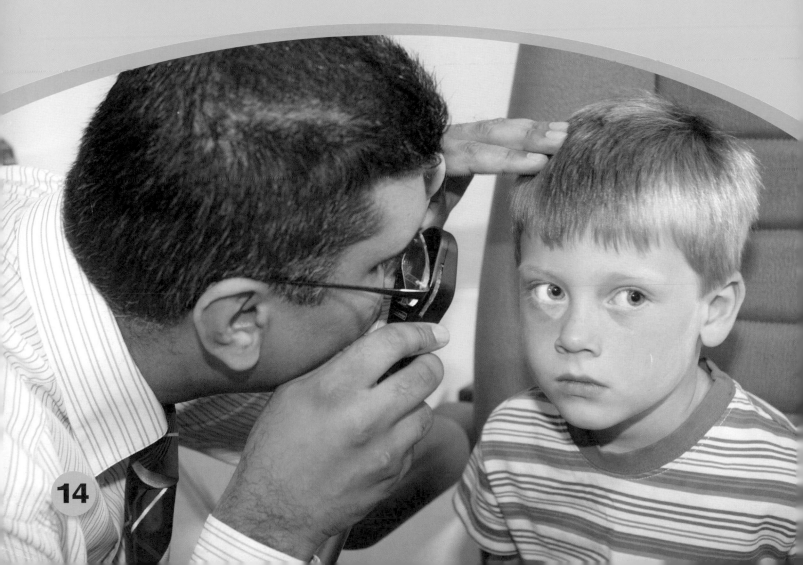

Sometimes, patients need **treatment** to help them with a problem. For example, they may wear special glasses to help correct a 'lazy eye'.

Do you know?

A lazy eye doesn't see as well as it should.

Choosing glasses

If a patient needs new glasses, we help them choose a pair that will suit them.

When they have chosen the **frames** they want, we make sure they fit properly. Then their lenses are fitted into the frames.

Do you know?

How many people in your family wear glasses?

Contact lenses

Many grown-ups wear **contact lenses** to help them see well.

What do you think?

Why do some people choose to wear contact lenses?

I give patients eye tests for contact lenses. I check that their eyes are healthy, and that the lenses they wear are comfortable.

Home visits

Sometimes I do home visits for patients who can't get out to the optician's for an eye test.

I take all my important
equipment with me in
a special case.

What do you think?

Why
might some
patients need
to be visited
at home?

Look after your eyes

Don't stare at bright lights, and never look straight at the Sun.

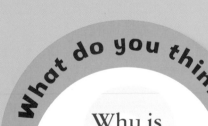

What do you think?

Why is looking after your eyes so important?

22

Visit the optician's regularly to find out
if you need new, or different, glasses.

Glossary

contact lenses small lenses that fit onto each eye to help you see

equipment the things you need to do something

eye test tests that an optician gives you to check how well you can see

frames a pair of glasses without the lenses in them

lenses pieces of glass or plastic which help people to see clearly

ophthalmoscope a piece of equipment that tests your eyesight

optician someone who tests eyesight and prepares glasses and contact glasses for people who need them

receptionist someone who works at a welcome desk

treatment care to help your eyesight get better

Index